Seeds of a Nation

Massachusetts

Don Nardo

KIDHAVEN PRESS™

THOMSON
————— ✦ —————
GALE

San Diego • Detroit • New York • San Francisco • Cleveland
New Haven, Conn. • Waterville, Maine • London • Munich

On cover: Pilgrims listen to the first sermon in Plymouth in 1621.

LIBRARY OF CONGRESS CATALOGING-IN-PUBLICATION DATA

Nardo, Don, 1947
    Massachusetts / by Don Nardo.
        p.cm.—(Seeds of a nation)
    Includes bibliographical references (p.   ) and index.
        ISBN 0-7377-1407-7
        1. Massachusetts—History—Colonial period, ca. 1600–1775—Juvenile literature.
    2. Massachusetts—History—1775–1865—Juvenile literature. [1. Massachusetts—History.] I. Title. II. Series.
        F67 .N37 2003
        974.4'02—dc21

                                                                    2002013596

Printed in China

Contents

Chapter One

Before the Coming of the Whites

M assachusetts is one of the oldest and most historic states in the Union. It became a state in 1788, following the American Revolution. But it already had a long history as one of the original thirteen British colonies. The term *Massachusetts* came from Massachuset, the name of a tribe of Native Americans who originally inhabited the area. In their language it meant "large hill place."

Massachusetts is a small state. Covering 10,555 square miles, it ranks only forty-fourth in size out of the fifty states. It is bordered in the north by New Hampshire and Vermont, in the west by New York, in the south by Connecticut and Rhode Island, and in the east by the Atlantic Ocean. An estimated 6.4 million people currently live in Massachusetts.

Communities of Farmers and Hunters

Of that total population, only about thirteen thousand people—less than 1 percent—are of Native American descent. Before the arrival of the first whites, all of the region's inhabitants were American Indians. Several distinct tribes occupied what is now Massachusetts. The Nauset lived on the beautiful peninsula of Cape Cod, which juts out into the Atlantic Ocean in the southeast. Small groups of Nauset also inhabited the nearby islands of Nantucket and Martha's Vineyard. Just west and north of Cape Cod, near the present town of Plymouth, dwelled the Wampanoag and Pokanoket. Moving farther

Drawings done by ancient Native Americans cover Dighton Rock, found in southeastern Massachusetts.

north, what is now Boston and areas east of it were the home of the Massachuset Indians. And in the central part of the future state lived the Nipmuc, in the north the Pennacook, and in the west the Pocomtuc.

All of these tribes belonged to a large Native American group called the Algonquian family. Each spoke a **dialect**, or slightly different version, of the Algonquian language. And all had similar lifestyles and customs.

The Algonquians lived in permanent villages in the forest. The average village had a population of about 250 men, women, and children. The villages were permanent because their inhabitants relied mainly on farming for food. Once farms had been established, there was no need to move from place to place following herds of game like other Native American tribes did.

Massachusetts's Place in the United States Today

A Native American hunter spears fish at the river's edge.

The village women tilled the soil, planted the seeds, and tended the crops. These crops were mainly vegetables such as corn, beans, and pumpkins.

Meanwhile, the men added to the crops by hunting and fishing. They caught perch, bass, and other small fish by jabbing them with spears. For larger fish, they sometimes used nets. Using bows and arrows, the village hunters killed moose and deer, as well as small game such as rabbits, birds, and turtles. Almost nothing was wasted. In addition to meat, these animals provided

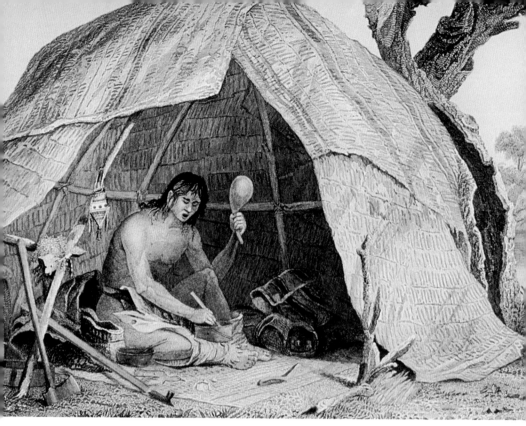

A dome-shaped wigwam provides shelter for a Native American medicine man.

skins for making clothes and shoes (**moccasins**), bones to use as needles and grinding tools, and tendons for making bow strings.

Shared Social Customs

The basis of social life in the Native American villages of Massachusetts was the family unit. A family was most often extended. It consisted not only of a father, mother, and children, but also grandparents, aunts, and other close relatives.

Families lived mainly in two kinds of houses. The first was the **wigwam**, a dome-shaped cabin. To construct it, builders drove two rows of poles into the ground so that they stood upright. Then they laid wide strips of bark over the poles to protect them from rain, sun, snow, and wind. The other type of home, the **longhouse**, was made in a similar manner. The difference was that a longhouse, as its name suggests, was much longer than a wigwam. In fact, some longhouses were large enough for two or three families to live in.

The children who lived in these houses did not attend formal schools. Instead, they learned from their parents and other village elders. Usually, women taught young girls to plant and harvest crops and to make clothes. And men taught young boys to hunt, fish, build houses, and fight.

Stories and Games

The children also learned about the world by listening to stories told by their elders. Such stories were often told during holiday festivals, in which the Indians thanked the spirits for providing corn and other natural gifts. Sometimes for days the Native Americans sang, danced, prayed, and played games. One of the most popular games played by the Wampanoag, Nauset, and other tribes in the region was similar to soccer. Players from one of two teams tried to kick a ball made of deerskin into the other team's goal.

Another custom the tribes of Massachusetts shared was the way they governed themselves. Most villages had a chief called a **sachem**. He did not have absolute power, like a king. Rather, he had to listen to and follow the advice of various village elders. Some were religious leaders, and others were heads of important local families.

Ravaged by War and Disease

One or more sachems led the tribe during wartime. Wars between different tribes were common in Massachusetts at the time. For example, the Massachuset and Wampanoag tribes were frequent rivals. The Massachuset also fought a Rhode Island tribe, the Narraganset.

Nineteenth-century warriors carry traditional spears, shields, and bow and arrows.

Before the Coming of the Whites

Warriors rarely formed large armies. Usually, small groups of fighters stalked one another in the forest, firing arrows from behind rocks and trees. In addition to the bow and arrow and spear, the most common weapon used in battle was a stone-headed club. On occasion, warriors from one tribe attacked and burned rival villages. Normally, few people died in these wars. So these conflicts did not wipe out entire peoples.

However, when combined with other factors, such wars did have an effect on native populations. One of these factors was the introduction of new diseases, including smallpox, by early European settlers. Disease and warfare ravaged the local Indians, especially the Massachuset tribe. In 1614 an estimated three thousand Massachuset lived in about twenty villages along the Charles and Neponset Rivers, near Boston. In the three years that followed, three disease **epidemics** swept through these villages and killed many people. Then, seeing their neighbors weakened, the Indians living north of the area attacked.

By 1629 only about five hundred Massachuset were left. And by 1640 most of the survivors lived in special villages set up by settlers. These villages were only for Native Americans who had converted to Christianity. Soon afterward the Massachuset ceased to exist as a separate people. All that was left was their name, preserved forever as the name of the whole region.

Chapter Two

Explorers, Fishermen, and Mapmakers

Native Americans had lived in Massachusetts and nearby areas for hundreds of generations. They had no idea that another land existed on the far side of the great sea that lapped their shores. Nor could they guess that people from that distant land would eventually cross the sea. Those visitors, with their lighter skins, strange customs, and lethal weapons, eventually built settlements. And soon the local Indians found themselves in a fight for survival.

However, well before the first people began settling the New England coast, numerous European ships sighted or landed in what is now Massachusetts. Some were explorers and mapmakers. Others were fishermen after the plentiful schools of cod and other fish in the coastal waters. So many ships of various kinds came and went over the years that it is difficult to tell who arrived first.

The Vikings on Cape Cod?

Some scholars think that the first white people who visited Massachusetts, and in fact North America in general, were the Vikings. They were hearty seafaring people who originally inhabited Denmark and Scandinavia. In the ninth and tenth centuries, they expanded into the northern Atlantic region. There they set up prosperous farming colonies in Ireland, Iceland, and Greenland.

A European ship makes its way across the Atlantic to New England.

According to epic tales passed down through the generations, sometime between A.D. 985 and 989, a Viking explorer named Bjarni Herjulfsson sailed southwest from Greenland. He sighted what are now Newfoundland and Nova Scotia, in southern Canada. He also saw a green strip of land that may have been Cape Cod. (Some historians argue that the land he saw was farther north, in Canada.) Herjulfsson sailed back to Greenland and described what he had seen.

Other Vikings were inspired by this tale of pleasant lands lying to the south. And a few years later a Viking named Leif Eriksson, sometimes called "Leif the Lucky,"

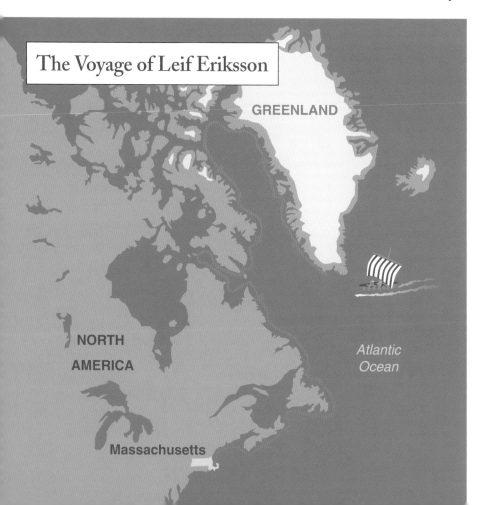

The Voyage of Leif Eriksson

GREENLAND

NORTH
AMERICA

Atlantic
Ocean

Massachusetts

A Viking trading ship embarks upon the sea for an expedition.

launched an expedition. He reached Cape Cod between 998 and 1002. According to the Viking epics, he found a river and sailed up it. This may have been the Bass River, located on the south side of Cape Cod. If so, Eriksson went to Follins Pond, lying between the present towns of Dennis and Yarmouth. There he stayed the winter. Then he returned to Greenland.

Next came Leif Eriksson's brother, Thorwald, who tried to establish a permanent settlement on Cape Cod. But for reasons unknown, Thorwald killed some local Indians, whom the Vikings called Skraelings. In response, a large band of Skraelings attacked the visitors and killed Thorwald. Still another Viking expedition followed, this one led by Thorfinn Karlsefni. He brought about 165 people to Cape Cod and established a colony. But because of continued troubles with the local natives, he abandoned the settlement three years later. That marked the end of Viking exploration of North America.

Many Fishermen and Traders

The next Europeans to reach Massachusetts were probably English or Portuguese fisherman. In 1497, English explorer John Cabot reached Newfoundland. He reported seeing huge schools of cod and other fish. In the years that followed, hundreds of fishing vessels made the dangerous journey across the ocean to cash in on this bounty. It is likely that at least some of them investigated the 750 miles of Massachusetts coastline.

A few of these early fishing expeditions involved entire fleets of vessels. In 1501, Gaspar Côrte-Real, a Portuguese nobleman, led such a fleet to Newfoundland to catch cod. But his ships were never heard from again. A year later his brother, Miguel, sailed with three ships to search for him. Miguel's expedition, like Gaspar's, never returned. However, centuries later some words were found carved into a rock near the mouth of the Taunton River, in southeastern Massachusetts. The message, written in Latin, reads: "M. Cortereal 1511 V. Dei Dux Ind." This translates as "M. Cortereal 1511 by God's grace the leader of the Indians." From this evidence historians conclude that Miguel was blown off course to the Massachusetts coast. And there he established relations with the natives, eventually becoming their chief.

Explorers, Fishermen, and Mapmakers

Throughout the 1500s small expeditions to New England continued. English, Spanish, Portuguese, French, Italian, and other fishermen and traders visited the coast of Massachusetts. However, none intended to settle there permanently. The aim was always to exploit the area's fish and other resources and sail home.

Well-wishers bid farewell to English explorer John Cabot.

Voyage of the *Concord*

It was not until 1602 that a European considered settling in Massachusetts. He was Bartholomew Gosnold, an English explorer and trader. With its crew of thirty-two, Gosnold's ship, the *Concord,* sailed down the coast of what is now Maine. Eventually the expedition landed on the tip of a peninsula shaped like a big fishhook. The nearby waters contained so much cod that Gosnold

Native Americans meet English explorer Bartholomew Gosnold with gifts on Cape Cod.

called the peninsula Cape Cod, the name it still bears today.

Next, Gosnold sailed southward and found a large island just off the southwestern coast of the Cape. He named the island Martha's Vineyard. Martha was his daughter's name. And the term vineyard referred to the plentiful wild grapevines growing there. A few miles northwest of Martha's Vineyard, Gosnold and his men found and named the Elizabeth Islands. On one of them, Cuttyhunk Island, they erected a fort and a house and planted some wheat and vegetables. The Englishmen also traded with the local Indians, whom they described as very peaceful and courteous.

Gosnold liked Massachusetts so much that he wanted to establish a large permanent colony there. He planned to leave twenty of his men to begin building a settlement. But he was running short of many supplies. So he sailed back to England, hoping to return in the near future.

Mapping the Coasts

After hearing about Gosnold's trip to the fertile lands of Massachusetts, a number of Europeans showed an interest in settling in the area. First, however, reliable maps had to be made. Otherwise future boatloads of settlers might become lost. In 1605 and again the following year, a French explorer, Samuel de Champlain, mapped the Massachusetts coast. He noted several sites that might be a suitable place to settle. Among them were Gloucester (north of Boston), Plymouth (south of Boston), and Eastham and Chatham (on Cape Cod).

English explorer John Smith mapped the Massachusetts coastline.

The Dutch also sent explorers to the area. In 1614, two of them, Adriaen Block and Hendrick Christiansen, charted the coasts of Massachusetts Bay. That same year, an Englishman, Captain John Smith, began mapping the coasts, bays, and river mouths of Massachusetts. It was Smith who named the general region New England. He also gave the area around Cape Cod the name of Massachusetts after the local Massachuset tribe.

After returning to England, Smith published *A Description of New England.* In it he provided a detailed summary of the terrain, plants, animals, and people of Massachusetts and nearby areas. The book was widely read in England and in other parts of Europe. And it soon inspired many people to move to Massachusetts.

Chapter Three

Building the First Settlements

M any English people read and enjoyed John Smith's book about the prospect of settling in New England. But two groups took a special interest. And these groups would establish the first permanent settlements in Massachusetts.

The two groups had much in common. Members of both opposed many of the practices of the Church of England. They believed the church had too many complicated ceremonies that had little or nothing to do with the Bible. They wanted to simplify and purify the church. So they became known as Puritans.

Though the two groups of Puritans had the same goals, they differed in their approach to achieving them. The first group chose to separate completely from the Church of England. For that reason they became known as the Separatists. However, openly opposing the church was a serious crime. So the Separatists worshiped in secret. Some were persecuted by the government and fled to the Netherlands. Because they knew what it was like to be harassed for their beliefs, they tended to be **tolerant,** or accepting of others' views.

By contrast, the second and larger group of Puritans decided to remain in the church and try to reform it from within. They saw themselves as the only truly pure Christians. And they were not at all tolerant of other faiths or religious viewpoints.

Pilgrims attend a church service at Plymouth Colony, Massachusetts.

The Mayflower *brought the Pilgrims across the Atlantic Ocean to Massachusetts.*

Voyage of the *Mayflower*

The Separatist group was the first of the two to sail for New England. The idea of starting fresh in a new, unspoiled land appealed to them. Early in 1620 some of them got permission from the English king to settle in New England. First, they journeyed to Plymouth, England. And there they joined a few dozen non-Separatists who also wanted to make the trip.

These travelers became known as the Pilgrims, a term that one of their leaders, William Bradford, saw in the Bible. At first they boarded two ships—the *Mayflower* and the *Speedwell*. However, the *Speedwell* soon began to leak and had to be abandoned. Having no other choice,

The Pilgrims land at Cape Cod after a two-month-long journey on the Mayflower.

all 102 Pilgrims crowded onto the *Mayflower,* which departed Plymouth on September 16, 1620.

Crossing the Atlantic Ocean took almost two months. The Pilgrims had planned to land near the Hudson River, in what is now New York. But the winds and tides took them to the shores of Cape Cod, in Massachusetts. With winter setting in, they did not want to risk another dangerous voyage. So they decided to stay. The ship anchored in the harbor at Province-town while some of the expedition's leaders explored the nearby coasts. On December 21, 1620, these men came ashore at what is now Plymouth. And five days later, the *Mayflower* arrived there.

From Hardship to Prosperity

The first winter was harsh and the Pilgrims suffered greatly. Some of the men worked long hours in freezing temperatures to cut down trees and build a small fort and a few modest houses. While waiting for these shelters, many of the settlers remained aboard the *Mayflower.* They, too, suffered from cold, as well as a lack of food. By the end of December six people had died. And by March 1621, only about fifty Pilgrims were still alive.

The situation improved in the spring, however. For several weeks the colonists noticed large numbers of Indians gathering nearby. Some Pilgrims feared the natives would attack. But these worries quickly faded. One day an Indian named Samoset walked into the colony and, in perfect English, welcomed the colonists. He had learned English from some fishermen in Maine.

Samoset was a friendly person, so he introduced the colonists to other Indians. Among them was Squanto, who had recently spent several years in England, where he, too, had learned to speak English. Squanto befriended the Pilgrims. He showed them the best places to fish and taught them how to grow corn. The colonists also made a treaty of friendship with Massasoit, chief of the Wampanoags.

Thanks to the Indians' help and the Pilgrims' own hard work, the colony began to thrive. In the autumn of 1621, the settlers decided to give thanks for their good fortune. They held a lavish celebration, which would become the annual Thanksgiving holiday in America. William Bradford, now governor of the colony, invited Massasoit, who attended with about ninety other Wampanoags. Everyone enjoyed a feast of wild turkey, deer, ducks, geese, fish, and corn.

Over the next few years, the colony continued to prosper. Other Separatists, as well as non-Separatists, arrived from England. The settlement became so crowded that some of the Pilgrims left and established new towns in the area. These included Duxbury, north of Plymouth, and Barnstable, on Cape Cod. By 1640 Plymouth Colony consisted of eight towns with a total population of about twenty-five hundred people.

The Pilgrims and the Wampanoag celebrate the first Thanksgiving in 1621.

The Massachusetts Bay Colony

The prosperity the Pilgrims enjoyed did not go unnoticed in England. While still at odds with the Church of England, a number of Puritans decided to make their own fortunes in Massachusetts. In 1628 a Puritan leader named John Endicott arrived with about fifty followers. They established a settlement at Salem, about fifty miles north of Plymouth. It became the first town in Massachusetts Bay Colony.

Two years later, about a thousand more Puritans, led by John Winthrop, arrived in Salem. However, the small settlement could not support that many people. So most of the new arrivals established new towns nearby. Among them were Dorchester, Watertown, and Medford. Winthrop led the largest group to a spot near the Charles River, about fifteen miles south of Salem. There they established Boston, named after the English town in which many of them had grown up. Between 1630 and 1640, another ten thousand Puritans joined the colony, most of whom settled in Boston.

Large numbers of the newcomers were children, which meant that schools were needed. The Puritans placed a strong emphasis on education. Puritan leaders believed that both men and women needed to be educated so that they could study the Bible. As a result of this belief, in 1635 they founded the first public school in America—Boston Latin School. They also established the first college in America—Harvard University—between 1636 and 1638.

A Puritan dissenter sits in the stocks as punishment for breaking the law.

Intolerance Leads to Trouble

Although the Puritans were open-minded about education, they were much less tolerant of **dissenting**, or differing or opposing, beliefs. Anyone who disagreed with the group's leaders, especially in religious matters, was treated as a lawbreaker. People who failed to attend church were whipped. Or they had to sit all day in **stocks**, wooden frameworks that trapped their hands

28

and feet. One dissenter, Salem resident Roger Williams, argued that people should be allowed to worship how and when they pleased. For this offense the colony's leaders banished him in 1635. After being banished, he started a new colony in nearby Rhode Island. Many other people were expelled from the colony simply for believing in religious freedom.

To the Puritans, even worse than the dissenters were the Indians, who were not even Christians. Some Puritans, including John Eliot, made an effort to convert local Indians to Puritan beliefs. Eliot erected special villages for these converts. The first village was in Natick, several miles west of Boston.

However, many other Puritans looked on the Indians as less than human. Puritans not only stole Indian

White settlers and Indians prepare to fight in King Philip's War.

land, but they also cheated Indians when trading with them. Relations with the Indians steadily worsened until violence finally erupted. In 1675, Metacomet, sachem of the Wampanoag, rallied tribes from the whole region to fight the settlers. The settlers called him Philip and the conflict King Philip's War. The fighting was intense and brutal. Hundreds of whites and thousands of Indians were killed before colonists from Massachusetts Bay, Plymouth, Connecticut, and Rhode Island crushed the uprising in 1676.

The act of joining forces for a common cause provided a hint of the future for the two Massachusetts colonies. Only fifteen years after Metacomet's defeat, the population of Plymouth was about ten thousand. And Massachusetts Bay had more than one hundred thousand people. Many residents of both colonies felt the time had come to unite as one.

Chapter Four

Protests, War, and Statehood

In the late 1600s, Plymouth Colony and Massachusetts Bay Colony combined as one colony, which eventually became a state. It was probably inevitable that the two colonies came together. Their inhabitants had long been in contact and traded with each other. And they had cooperated in fighting Indians during King Philip's War.

The Issue of Free Trade

In the late 1600s the colonies had a new reason to work together. They had grown very prosperous over the years. And they exported many valuable goods to England. Among these were cod and other fish, corn and other crops, animal furs, cloth and clothes, iron, lumber, shoes, and candles. The colonists wanted to trade these goods with other countries in addition to trading with

England. But England wanted to retain a **monopoly**, or sole possession, of the trade. To gain total control, England's legislature, **Parliament**, passed the Navigation Acts. These laws made it illegal for the colonies to trade with other countries.

A Massachusetts Bay Colony windmill overlooks the coast in this 1630s scene.

But the colonists felt the new laws interfered with their personal freedom. So they ignored the Navigation Acts and began smuggling products out of Boston and other ports. In 1684 the angry British king, Charles II, responded. He took away Massachusetts Bay Colony's right to govern itself. Two years later Charles's successor, James II, sent a royal governor to rule Massachusetts and the other colonies in New England.

Luckily for the colonists, the situation improved somewhat under the next British rulers—William III and Mary II. In 1691 they combined Plymouth Colony and Massachusetts Bay Colony into Massachusetts Colony. The new capital was Boston. The colony was allowed to have its own legislature, with its members elected by the people. However, a royal governor still ruled. And he could **veto**, or stop passage of, any law the colonists made.

Years of Rapid Growth

The new Massachusetts Colony prospered and grew rapidly. By 1765 its population surpassed 250,000. Of these, 20,000 lived in Boston, then the largest city in all of England's thirteen American colonies. About 80 percent of the inhabitants were of English descent. The rest were a mix of French, Canadians, Scots, Irish, Germans, and a few black Africans, some slaves and some free. Religion was also becoming more diverse. Some people still followed the old Puritan beliefs. But many colonists belonged to the Church of England. And Catholics and Quakers were common, too.

An engraving depicts Boston Common as it might have looked in the 1660s.

Churches for these faiths sprang up in communities across the colony. So did courthouses and other public buildings, shops, and many new homes. Usually the majority of these structures clustered around a central town square or public park called a common. The large one in Boston became known as Boston Common.

In the **rural** areas, or the countryside, the town centers were surrounded by farmland. Farming was the main profession outside the big cities. In the cities most people were shopkeepers, fishermen, or dock laborers. Thousands of ships, carrying goods from around the world, docked at Boston's port each year. In addition, two other Massachusetts ports—Nantucket and New Bedford—were the leading whaling centers of North America.

The Road to Independence

Although Massachusetts was prosperous by the 1760s, it also became a center of political unrest in these same years. Any significant increase in taxes hurt merchants and farmers alike. So when England began imposing new taxes, the colonists protested.

The trouble increased in 1765. England had recently been involved in a major conflict with France. Known as the French and Indian War, it had ended in 1763 with a British victory. British leaders wanted to keep their army large in case the French started another war. To equip and pay these troops, Parliament decided to tax the American colonies. In 1765 it passed the Stamp Act, which forced the colonists to pay taxes on newspapers, pamphlets, and other paper products.

Reaction to the Stamp Act in Massachusetts was loud and sometimes violent. Enraged citizens in Boston

American colonists burn stamps in protest of the British Stamp Act.

destroyed the homes of local tax collectors. Meanwhile, the legislature pondered what to do about the new taxes. It decided to join with the legislatures of the other British colonies in issuing a formal protest. The colonists argued that they had no representatives in Parliament to support and defend their interests. It was therefore unfair for Parliament to impose its will on them.

British leaders gave in and **repealed**, or canceled, the Stamp Act in 1766. But they soon imposed new taxes on Massachusetts and the other colonies. One of these taxes was on tea. To protest, in December 1773 a gang of Boston men dressed up like Indians. They went to the local docks and dumped 342 chests of British tea into the harbor. This event became known as the Boston Tea Party. This time the British were the ones who were angry. They closed the port of Boston and forced local citizens to let British troops live in their homes.

These and other events eventually led to armed rebellion, which turned out to be the first major step in Massachusetts becoming a state. The first battles of the American Revolution took place in the villages of Lexington and Concord, not far from Boston, in April 1775. The following year representatives from Massachusetts and the other colonies met in Philadelphia. On July 4 they issued the Declaration of Independence, which created a new nation. In 1781, after several years of war, that new nation, the United States, defeated England.

The Sixth State

While fighting the war for independence, the leaders of the thirteen colonies had given much thought to what

Colonists dressed as Indians dump British tea into the harbor at the Boston Tea Party.

would happen if they won the conflict. Not only would they have a new country, but each of the former colonies would become a state in that country. Also, those states would have to agree on what form the new nation's government would take.

In the years following the American victory in 1781, representatives from the former colonies met on several occasions to discuss these matters. They eventually decided that they needed to create a **constitution**, a new set of rules for governing the country. The representatives met in Philadelphia in May 1787 to begin drawing up the Constitution. In September they sent the finished product to the legislatures of the former colonies. Each

Boston today is a mix of modern high-rises and historic sites.

legislature met and studied the document, and its members voted on whether or not to accept it. By accepting the Constitution, a former colony officially became a state in the new nation. Massachusetts agreed to accept the U.S. Constitution on February 6, 1788, and it became the sixth state.

Ever since that time, Massachusetts has made enormous contributions to the country. Four of its native sons have served as president of the United States—John Adams, John Quincy Adams, Calvin Coolidge, and John F. Kennedy. Boston remains one of the nation's greatest cities. And each year tens of thousands of people come to see the historic places where America's struggle for independence began.

Facts About Massachusetts

Admitted to Union: February 6, 1788

State capital: Boston

State nicknames: the Bay State, and the Old Colony State

State motto: "By the sword we seek peace, but peace only under liberty"

State flower: mayflower

State bird: black-capped chickadee

State fish: cod

State tree: American elm

State berry: cranberry

State marine mammal: right whale

State dog: Boston terrier

State folk hero: Johnny Appleseed

State song: "All Hail to Massachusetts," adopted in 1981

2002 population: 6.4 million

Largest cities: Boston (population 600,000), Worcester (180,000), Springfield (155,000), Lowell (108,000)

Smallest town: Gosnold (86)

Number of counties: 14

Total area: 10,555 square miles

Land area: 7,838 square miles

Water area: 2,717 square miles

Largest lake: Quabbin Reservoir (24,704 acres)

Highest point: Mount Greylock (3,491 feet), in Pittsfield

Lowest point: sea level, on the Atlantic coast

Average temperatures in Boston: 28 degrees in January; 72 degrees in July

Per capita income in 2002: $38,000

Principal manufactured products: electronic machinery, computer equipment, chemicals, transportation equipment

Principal agricultural products: milk, nursery and greenhouse products, eggs, vegetables, cranberries

Principal minerals: clay, lime, marble, sand and gravel, quartz, granite

Glossary

constitution: A set of rules for governing a state, country, or other political unit.

dialect: A slightly different version of a language.

dissenting: Differing from or opposing the norm.

epidemics: Outbreaks of diseases that kill many people.

longhouse: A large, oblong dwelling constructed from wooden poles and strips of bark.

moccasins: Shoes made of animals skins, worn by members of many Native American tribes.

monopoly: Sole possession or control over something.

Parliament: The legislature of Great Britain.

repealed: Canceled.

rural: Having to do with the countryside.

sachem: A village chief in many Native American tribes that inhabited the area of Massachusetts.

stocks: A device used to punish lawbreakers in colonial America; it consisted of a wooden framework that trapped a person's hands and feet.

tolerant: Understanding and accepting of others' views. Someone who is not understanding and accepting is said to be intolerant.

veto: To reject or stop passage of a law.

wigwam: A small, domelike dwelling constructed from wooden poles and strips of bark.

For Further Exploration

Carolyn Croll, *The Story of the Pilgrims.* New York: Random House, 1995. A concise look at the English settlers who founded Plymouth Colony in Massachusetts.

Stuart A. Kallen, *Native Americans of the Northeast.* San Diego: Lucent Books, 2000. Tells the story of the various Indian tribes that inhabited Massachusetts and neighboring areas before and after the coming of Europeans. Written for junior high school readers.

Deborah Kent, *Lexington and Concord.* Danbury, CT: Childrens Press, 1997. Aimed at young readers, this is an excellent overview of the opening battles of the American Revolution.

Allison Lassieur, *Before the Storm: American Indians Before the Europeans.* New York: Facts On File, 1998. A look at Indian life and customs right before European colonization.

Don Nardo, *The American Revolution.* San Diego: KidHaven Press, 2003. A summary of the conflict between England and its American colonies.

Walter Olesky, *The Boston Tea Party.* New York: Franklin Watts, 1993. The events and personalities shaping this famous incident are told here in a simple format for basic readers.

Kathleen Thompson, *Massachusetts.* New York: Raintree/Steck-Vaughn, 1996. A well-written overview of the history and resources of the state.

For Further Exploration

Kate Waters, *Tapenum's Day: A Wampanoag Indian Boy in Pilgrim Times*. New York: Scholastic, 1996. Though the story is fictional, this volume has been carefully researched and presents an accurate picture of Native American life in seventeenth-century Massachusetts.

Susan Whitehurst, *The Colony of Massachusetts*. New York: Powerkids Press, 2000. An informative summary of the founding and life of the colony.

Index

Index

Picture Credits

About the Author

Historian and award-winning author Don Nardo has written many books for young people about American history, including *The American Revolution*, *The Mexican-American War*, *The Declaration of Independence*, and biographies of presidents Thomas Jefferson, Andrew Johnson, and Franklin D. Roosevelt. Mr. Nardo lives with his wife Christine in Massachusetts.